THE BUZZ

BEE

BOOK for KIDS

Storybook, Bee Facts, and Activities!

Alice B. McGinty

ROCKRIDGE PRESS

For general information on our other products and services or to obtain technical support, please contact our Customer Care Department within the United States at (866) 744-2665, or outside the United States at (510) 253-0500.

Rockridge Press publishes its books in a variety of electronic and print formats. Some content that appears in print may not be available in electronic books, and vice versa.

Series Designer: Stephanie Sumulong
Interior and Cover Designer: Angela Navarra
Art Producer: Sue Bischofberger
Editor: Laura Bryn Sisson
Production Editor: Nora Milman
Production Manager: Holly Haydash

Cover and interior photography licensed courtesy of Science Source, Alamy, iStock and Shutterstock.
Author photo courtesy Jon Dessen.

Paperback ISBN: 978-1-63807-451-9 | eBook ISBN: 978-1-63807-248-5
R0

Peekaboo! I'm Buzzy Bee! I live inside this hive.

We honeybees say, "Come on in!"

Fact:
Honeybees build their hives on tree branches, inside tree trunks, and even underground. A colony of more than 60,000 bees can live inside one hive!

It's buzzing and alive!

The queen bee lays her eggs in cells.
That's how each bee begins.
Then out hatch larvae, small and white,

that eat and grow and spin!

Fact:
What do the larvae spin? Cocoons! After being fed royal jelly and growing for four to seven days, larvae make cocoons for themselves and worker bees seal their cells.

Fact:
In that sealed cell, the pupa molts, meaning it sheds its old skin and changes. The bee that emerges is a fully grown adult.

The bee becomes a pupa now,
with legs and wings and eyes.

It chews out in a week or two,
and now it's grown in size.

Who says we bees all look the same?
I'll tell you who is who.

The queen, the drones, the worker bees—
we all have jobs to do!

Fact:
There's only one queen bee per hive. She is larger than the rest and has the most important job—laying up to 2,000 eggs per day!

Fact:
Drones have big eyes
and large, thick bodies
with no stingers—the
drones rarely leave
the hive.

These drones, they're males with just one job—
mating with the queen.

The rest, like me, are worker bees.

We build. We feed. We clean!

As days go by, we worker bees grow into other jobs.

We feed and groom the queen and drones.

These bees can sure be slobs!

Fact:
Worker bees change jobs as they age. At around two weeks old, their bodies begin making wax, which they use to build and repair the hive.

Fact:
Once a worker bee's stinger develops, she guards the hive against bees from other colonies, hornets, ants, and bears who are after honey and larvae.

Finally, I get to fly—
to go in search of food.

But wait! I see a predator.
I must protect the brood!

A flower! Nectar! Warm and sweet.
I suck it with my tongue.

I must collect a LOT of food,
while I'm still fit and young.

Fact:
Worker bees start foraging for food at three weeks old and will only live a few more weeks. They'll visit 50 to 200 flowers per trip.

Tiny grains of pollen
are the other food I need.

They stick onto my fuzzy hairs,
and some have fallen free.

Fact:
Pollen that falls from a bee onto another flower will pollinate it, allowing the flower to reproduce. Bees are important pollinators whose work allows many fruits and vegetables to grow!

Flowers, flowers everywhere!
This garden tastes so yummy!
I pack the pollen on my legs
and nectar in my tummy!

Fact:
Bees have special honey stomachs to carry their nectar. A bee can tote a load of nectar and pollen weighing as much as its whole body.

My tummy's full. I'm heading home—
with lots of things to share.

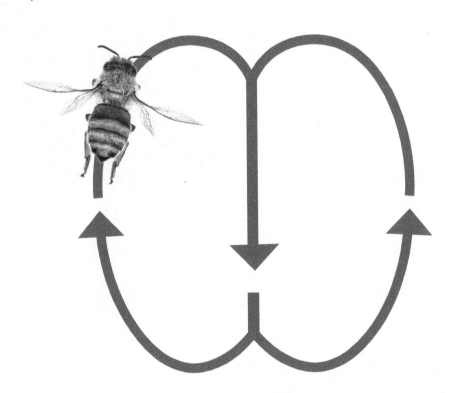

I'll tell my friends about these blooms,
and dance to show them where!

Fact:
Bees do the waggle dance to communicate where the best flowers are. Wiggling their abdomens, they walk in circles to show distance and direction.

It's time to feed the little ones
so they can grow up strong.
Another job for busy me—
my days are very long!

Fact:
Workers combine pollen and honey to make protein-rich "bee bread," which they feed to the larvae. They check on the larvae more than 1,000 times per day!

We found the food. We fed our young.
But work is STILL not done.

We'll make honey every day
to store for everyone.

Fact:
Worker bees make honey by drying nectar. They spit out the nectar, then help it to dry by flapping their wings.

Winter's coming very soon.
Is there enough to eat?

We must save up our honey
to survive 'til springtime's heat.

Fact:
In the winter, the bees survive on honey. To conserve it, they make the drones leave the hive, because the drones' only job is done.

Gather 'round and warm the queen.
Protect her from the cold!

But that job's for the younger bees.
I'm tired and I'm old.

Fact:
The colony clusters together, vibrating, with the queen at the center to warm her through the winter so she can lay eggs in spring.

Hey, look! Another worker bee. She's poking out her head!

Fact:
Because worker bees work so hard, they live for only five to six weeks. New bees hatch and take over their busy jobs!

There's lots and lots of work to do—a BUZZY life ahead!

BUZZY BONUS
GAMES & ACTIVITIES

Where's the Hive?

Lead Buzzy Bee to the hive.

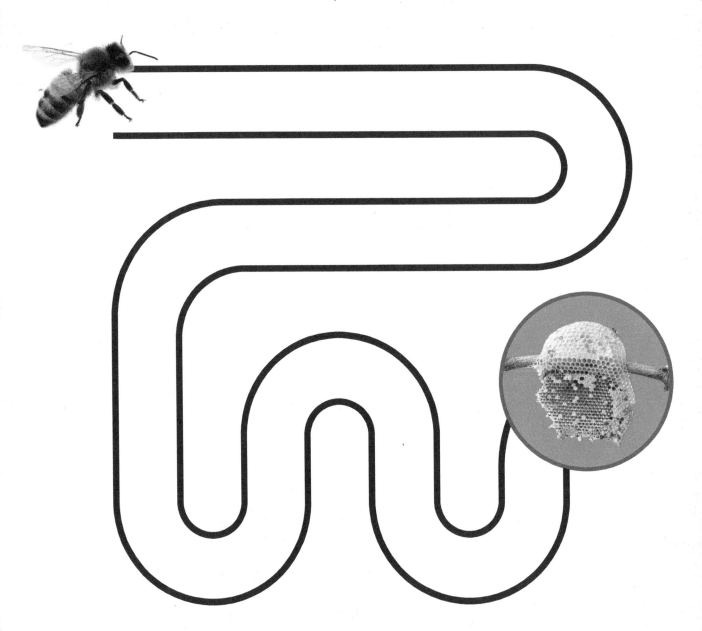

Which Job?

Write an X on the job that is not for a worker bee.

Fan the hive.

Drive a car.

Feed the larvae.

Collect nectar.

Find the Queen

Which one is the queen bee? Circle her!

What Comes Next?

Draw lines to match the pictures to the right stage of a bee's life.

larva

adult

pupa

egg

Help Buzzy Bee!

Which path leads Buzzy Bee to the flower?

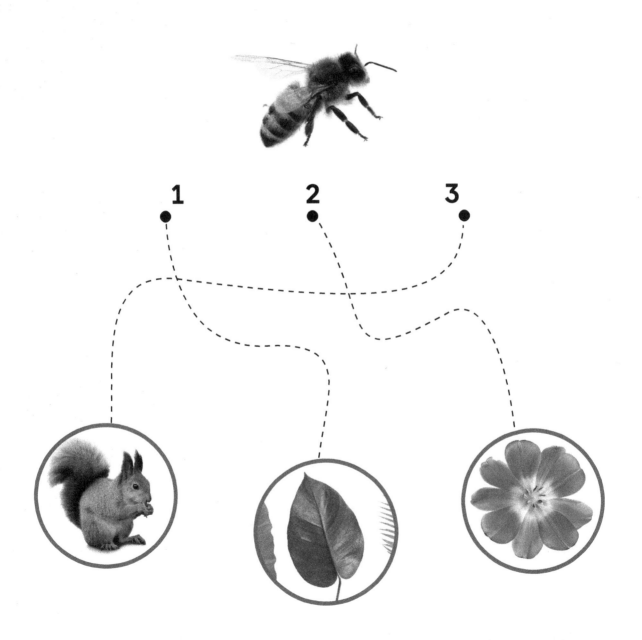

Make a Match

Match the words to the pictures.

flower

bee

hive

honey

Find the Garden

Lead Buzzy Bee through the maze to the garden.

Which Food?

Which of these foods do we get from bees? Circle the right one!

Find the Bees!

There are six bees hiding in this garden.
Find them and circle them.

Do the Waggle Dance

Show the bee how to do the waggle dance.
Follow the arrows to draw the path.

Repair the Hive!

What does Buzzy Bee use to repair the hive?
Draw a line to the answer.

wax

duct tape

wood

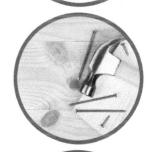

glue

Answer Key

Where's the Hive?
Lead Buzzy Bee to the hive.

Which Job?
Write an X on the job that is not for a worker bee.

Fan the hive.

Drive a car.

Feed the larvae.

Collect nectar.

Find the Queen
Which one is the queen bee? Circle her!

What Comes Next?
Draw lines to match the pictures to the right stage of a bee's life.

larva

adult

pupa

egg

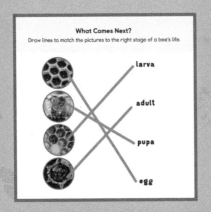

Help Buzzy Bee!
Which path leads Buzzy Bee to the flower?

1   2   3

Make a Match
Match the words to the pictures.

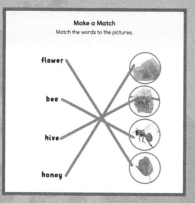

flower

bee

hive

honey

Find the Garden
Lead Buzzy Bee through the maze to the garden.

Which Food?
Which of these foods do we get from bees? Circle the right one!

Find the Bees!
There are six bees hiding in this garden.
Find them and circle them.

Do the Waggle Dance
Show the bee how to do the waggle dance.
Follow the arrows to draw the path.

Repair the Hive!
What does Buzzy Bee use to repair the hive?
Draw a line to the answer.

wax

duct tape

wood

glue

About the Author

Alice B. McGinty delights in igniting minds and imaginations. As the award-winning author of almost 50 children's books, including one of *Kirkus Reviews*' Best of 2020, *A Story for Small Bear* (Schwartz & Wade Books, illustrated by Richard Jones), and 2019 Northern Lights Book Award winner (food category) *Pancakes to Parathas: Breakfast Around the World* (Little Bee Books, illustrated by Tomoko Suzuki), she makes fiction and nonfiction accessible, engaging, and fun.

CPSIA information can be obtained
at www.ICGtesting.com
Printed in the USA
JSHW010037180821
17950JS00006B/60